Cool-Doo Math

[GRADE 1 AND 2]

Bound Volume

(Vol.01 - Vol.04)

www.cool-doo.com

01

Word Problems by Peter Feng
Comic Stories by Andrew Feng
Comic Sketches by Andrew Feng
Digital Ink by Peter Feng

First Printing: 2015

ISBN: 978-0-9938371-1-1

www.cool-doo.com

Number
rules the universe.

- Pythagoras (569-500BC)

Jack

Cool-Doo

Sleepy-Doo

To know the adventure of Jack and his gang,
please read *TUM* - The Unmoved Mover.
www.t-u-m.net

Dr. Green

Dr. Z

Jr. Z

To know the adventure of Jack and his gang,
please read *TUM* - The Unmoved Mover.
www.t-u-m.net

Contents

Jack's Chips vs Cool-Doo's Chips

ANSWER

SOLUTION

Jack has 16 bags of chips, but he lost 4 of them, so he has 12 bags left.

Cool-Doo has 14 bags of chips, but he only lost 1 of them, so he has 13 bags left.

Therefore, Cool-Doo has 1 more bag than Jack.

The correct answer is C.

ANSWER

SOLUTION

You need to add up Jack's coins first:
$2 + $1 + 25¢ × 8 + 20¢ = $5 and 20¢.

A TUM Lollipop is $5 and 11¢,
so do $5 and 20¢ - $5 and 11¢ = 9¢,
which is the change.

The correct answer is A.

What's the Time?

SMASH!

SMASH!

SMASH!

Why didn't I get one for Christmas?

THIS HOVERBOARD CAN DO ANYTHING!

ANSWER

SOLUTION

First, you need to read the clock when Jack gets to school. It says 8:35.

Jack also says that he takes 30 minutes to walk to school.

So, you have to subtract 30 minutes from 8:35, which is 8:05

The correct answer is C.

Sleepy-Doo's Password 1,2,3,4,5...

ANSWER

SOLUTION

You have to find the pattern of
Sleepy-Doo's first 4 numbers:
23, 26, 29, 32.

What's the pattern?
Is it counting by 1?
Nope.

How about 2?
Nuh-uh.

3?
Yes!

So, the next number in the password
should be 32+ 3 = 35.

The correct answer is B.

What is the Temperature ?

Dr.Green was testing his new thermometer with Jack.
50
40
30
20
10
0
10
20
30
40
MONDAY
Awesome invention! It looks like a candy tree!
Is that a good temperature for a trip?

ANSWER

SOLUTION

Look at the thermometre representing Monday's temperature in the first page. It reads 30 °C.

In the next page, the thermometre representing Tuesday's temperature is blocked by clouds, but Dr.Green says that it is 10 °C lower than Monday's temperature.

So, to figure out Tuesday's temerature, just do 30 °C - 10 °C = 20 °C.

The correct answer is C.

Chip "BARS"

I find out
that I have
20 original chips,
15 cheddar chips,
and 10 spicy chips.

SPICY!

If I put this information on a bar graph, what should it look like?
How about this?

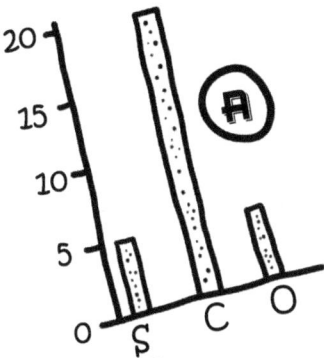
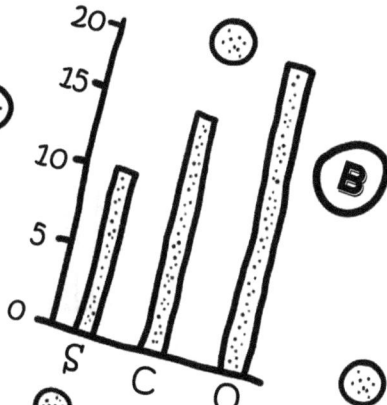
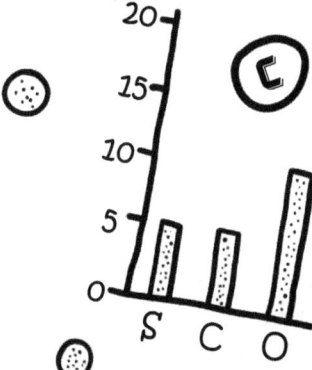
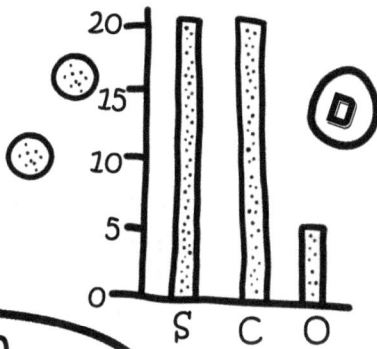

ANSWER

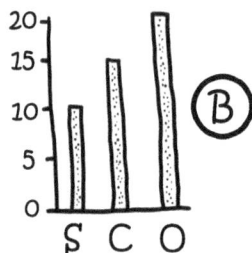

SOLUTION

Jack says that he has 10 spicy chips, 15 cheddar chips, and 20 original chips.

On the bar graph, the spicy chips should be 10 units high, the cheddar chips should be 15 units high, and the original chips should be 20 units high.

The correct answer is B.

Cool-Doo's Sunglasses

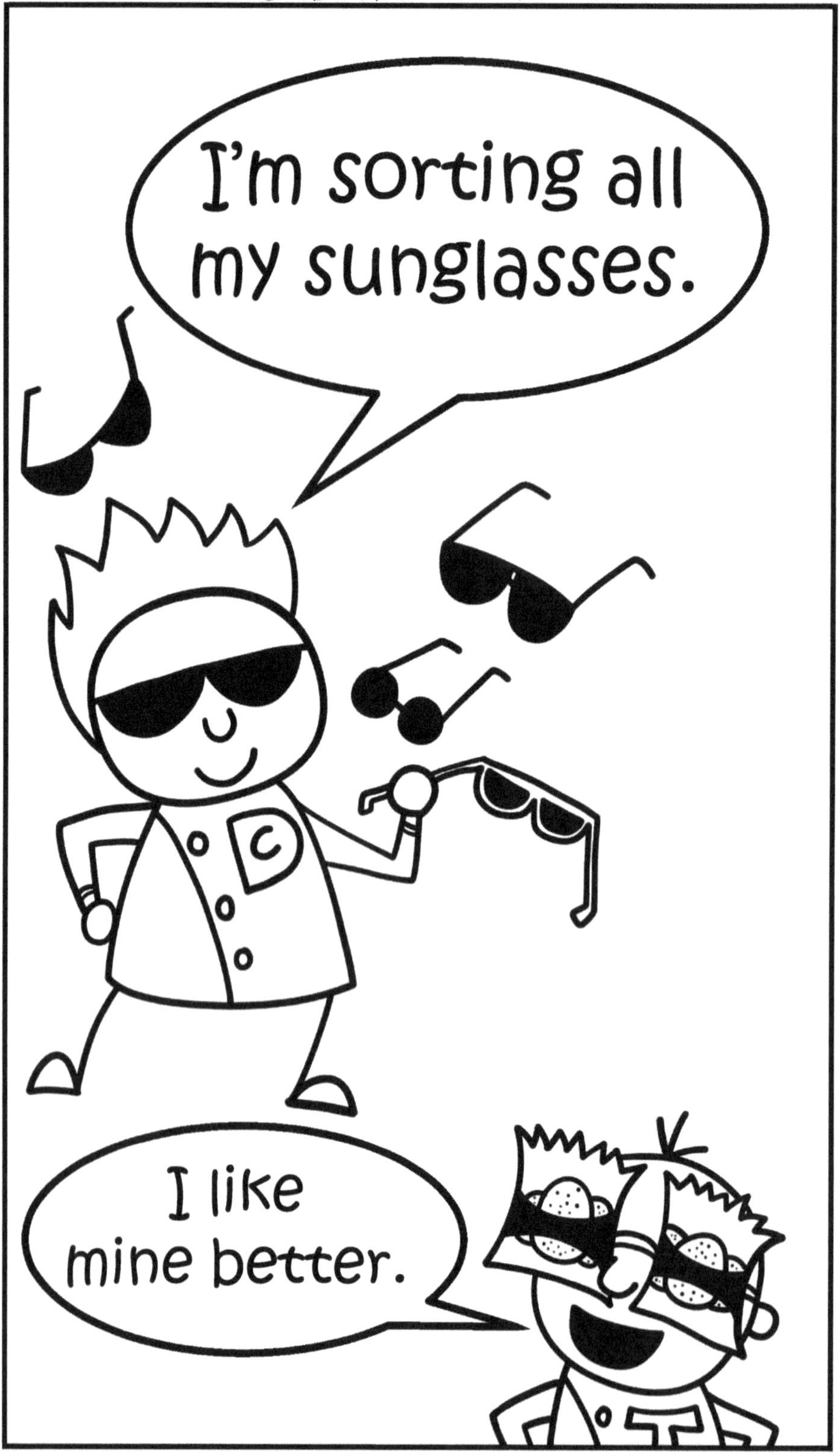
I'm sorting all my sunglasses.
I like mine better.

ANSWER

SOLUTION

First, you have to count how many pairs of sunglasses Cool-Doo has.

He has 9 pairs of sunglasses. Then, you count the number of pairs of the sunglasses with the same type that he wants you to sort.

There is only 1 pair of that kind.

So, the fraction is 1/9.

The correct answer is C.

Sleepy-Doo's Pillows

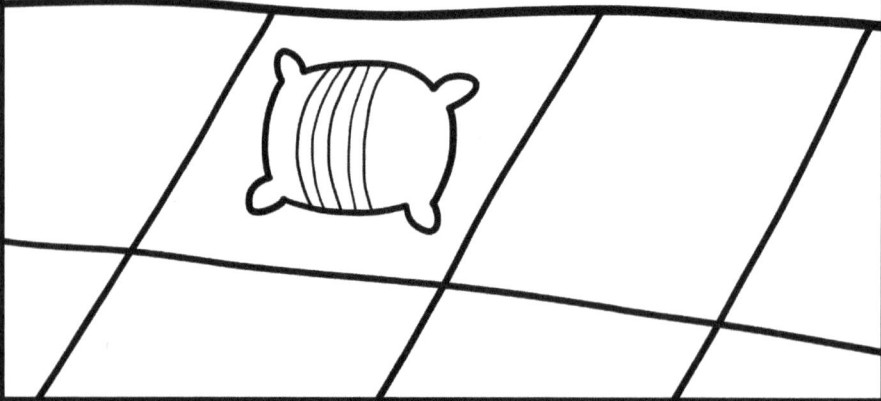

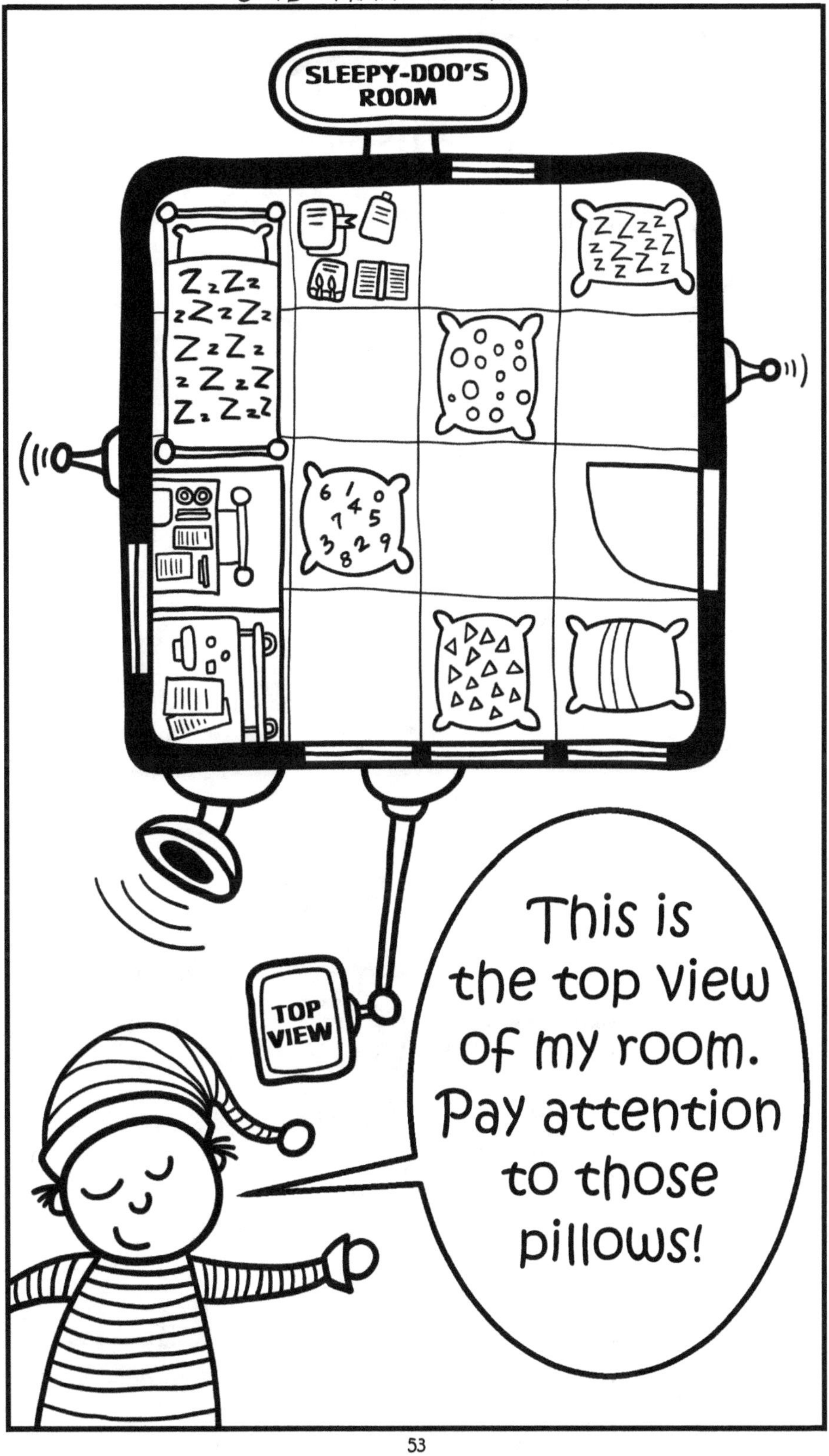
SLEEPY-DOO'S ROOM
TOP VIEW
This is the top view of my room. Pay attention to those pillows!

ANSWER

SOLUTION

Sleepy-Doo asks for the pillow that is on the top right of his bedroom.

Find the very top of the grid, then locate the tile on the right.

The pillow on that tile is your answer.

The correct answer is D.

ATTACKING the MOLES

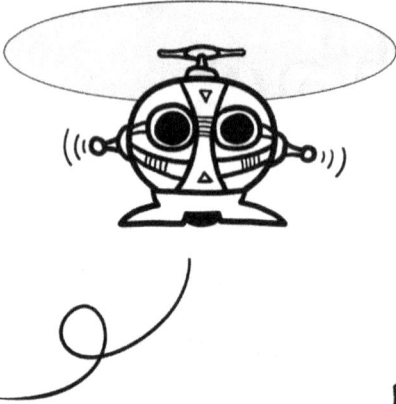

ANSWER

SOLUTION

Jr. Z says that he *aims* at 5 robot moles in the 1st round. That doesn't mean he hits 5 moles.

Actually he misses one, so he only hits 4 moles.

Altogether, Jr. Z hits 14 moles in the 2 rounds.

To figure out how many robot moles he hits in the 2nd round, do 14 - 4 = 10.

The correct answer is C.

Making TUM CHiPS

ANSWER

SOLUTION

If each bowl can fit 10 potatoes, 4 bowls can fit 40 potatoes. But there are still 5 potatoes left, so you still need 1 more bowl for these 5 potatoes.

Therefore, Jack needs 5 bowls.

The correct answer is D.

What Will I Take Out?

A Eat one bag of TUM Chips.

B Clean Cool-Doo's room.

C Take out the trash.

D Wash dishes.

Jack, you have to take out a tag from this bag without looking. Each tag has a letter on it. Take a look at the chart above!

TUM Chips! TUM Chips!

Bad Idea, Jack!

Hee hee hee!
I put 20 Bs, 7 Cs,
4 Ds, and only 1 A!
Good luck,
Jack.
Ha ha ha!

Please take
TUM Chips!
Please take
TUM Chips...

Jack, you are
in big trouble...

ANSWER

SOLUTION

Cool-Doo has put tag B in the bag 20 times, more than any other tags he put there.

So, Jack will most likely take tag B, which says to clean Cool-Doo's room.

The correct answer is B.

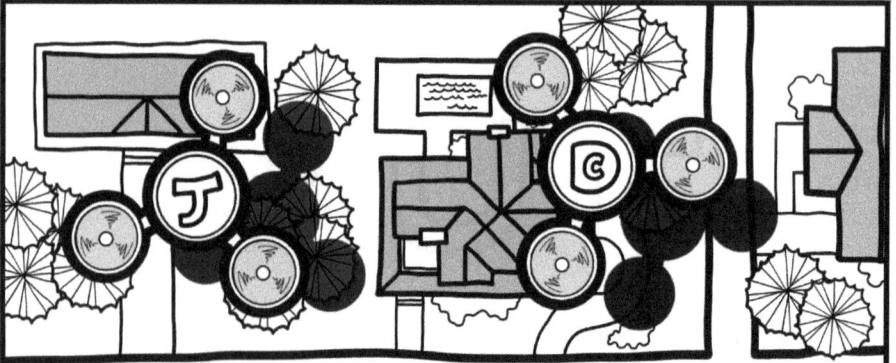

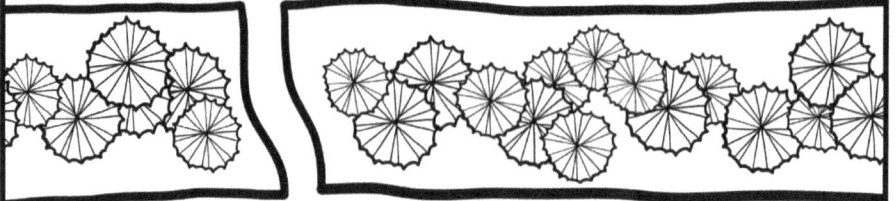

TUM-GPS

Jack, Cool-Doo and
Sleepy-Doo were delivering
pizzas with TUMCOPTERS!

They earned **$2.00** for each pizza they delivered.

Jack delivered **10** pizzas.

Cool-Doo delivered **5** pizzas.

Sleepy-Doo delivered **2** pizzas.

ANSWER

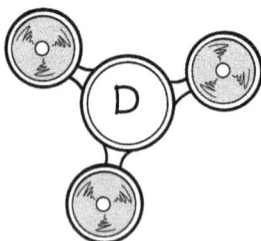

D

SOLUTION

Jack delivers 10 pizzas and each one costs $2.00, so $2.00 × 10 = $20.00.

Sleepy-Doo delivers 2 pizzas, so $2.00 × 2 = $4.00.

Cool-Doo delivers 5 pizzas, so $2.00 × 5 = $10.00.

Now, add these! $20.00 + $4.00 + $10.00 = $34.00.

The correct answer is D.

How Long is the "Canal"?

We're playing on the beach. We build 2 sand castles and a canal between them. Also, we constructed 2 bridges.

The distance between Crab Castle and Dolphin Bridge is 5 sailboats.

The distance between Dolphin Bridge and Seahorse Bridge is 12 sailboats.

A

30 sailboats

B

17 sailboats

C

18 sailboats

D

25 sailboats

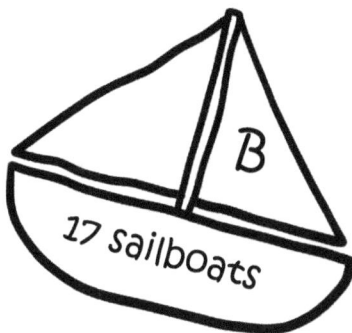

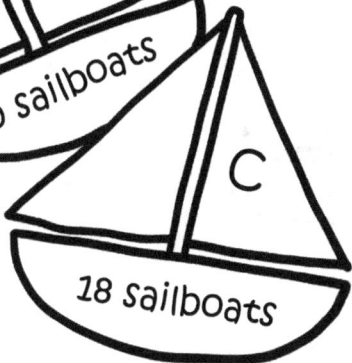

Boom! Splash!
TUM Sailboat
Fight!
Bam! Whoosh!

TUM

TUM

TUM

ANSWER

SOLUTION

All you have to do for this question is add all of the distances.

5 sailboats + 12 sailboats + 13 sailboats = 30 sailboats.

The correct answer is A.

Fish, Turtles, and Froggs

ANSWER

SOLUTION

First, to figure out the number of legs all 6 turtles have, do 4 legs × 6 turtles = 24 legs because each turtle has 4 legs.

Now, this is the tricky part - the 11 fish don't have any legs! So, you don't have to do anything here.

Finally, each frog has 4 legs, so 4 legs × 4 frogs = 16 legs.

Now, add up the 2 numbers.
24 legs + 16 legs = 40 legs.

The correct answer is C.

ANSWER

SOLUTION

Jack has already finished making 3 houses. He needs to make 7 more.

Each house is made of 8 sticks, but the connected houses share 1 stick. So, each additional house only needs 7 sticks.

$7 \times 7 = 49$.

The correct answer is D.

Removing TUM CHiPS

ANSWER

SOLUTION

Jack's board has 4 rows and 4 columns. Since each row and column only have one chip, there are only 4 chips needed to be left on the board.

Altogether, there are 11 chips on the board now, so 11 - 4 = 7, which is the number of chips needed to be removed.

The correct answer is B.

How Many Pillows?

Cool-Doo and Sleepy-Doo are comparing each other's pillows.

Altogether we have 54 pillows.
How many pillows does Cool-Doo have?
Hmff...

ANSWER

SOLUTION

If subtracting 50 pillows from the total 54 pillows, there are only 4 pillows left, and now Cool-Doo and Sleepy-Doo have the same number of pillows.

So, Cool-Doo has 2 pillows, which is half of 4 pillows.

The correct answer is C.

Building a TUM Land

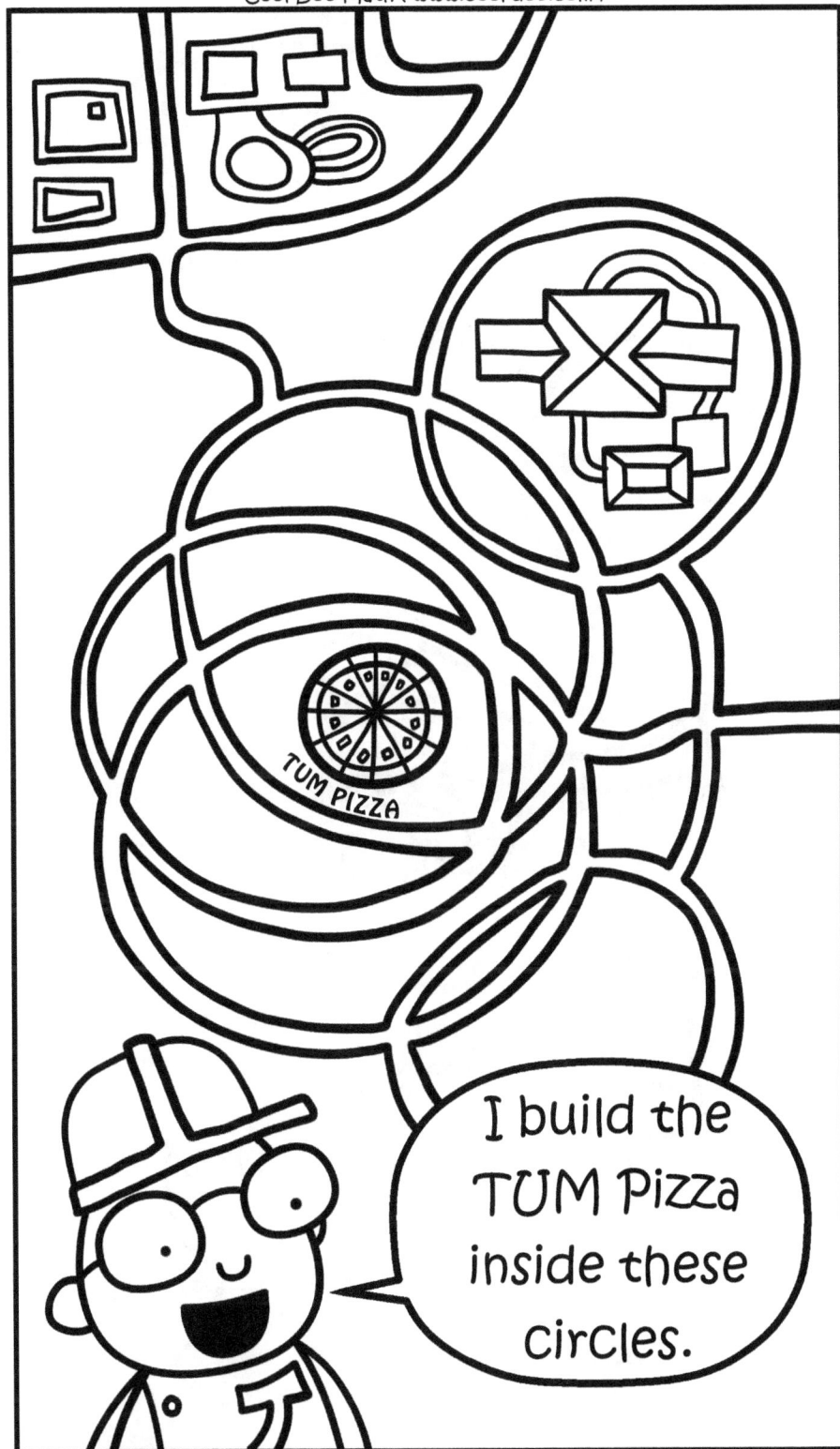

ANSWER

SOLUTION

All you have to do is to count the number of circles the TUM Pizza is in.

However, watch out for the overlapping circles. Count carefully!

The correct answer is D.

Pod Racing

Jack and Cool-Doo were choosing their space pods for a race.

Each pod had its own colour.

I want that one!

No, I want that one!

The blue pod is in front of pod #4, but behind pod #1.

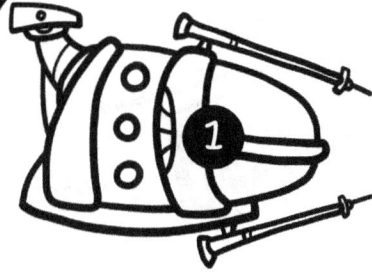

The red pod is behind the blue pod.

The green pod is in front of the blue pod, but it is not the 1st pod.

The black pod is behind the blue pod.

The black pod is in front of the red pod.

ANSWER

SOLUTION

For this question, you have to follow the instructions.

The blue pod must be either Pod 2 or Pod 3, since it is between Pod 1 and Pod 4.

The green pod is not the first one, but it is in front of the blue pod. That means the green pod must be Pod 2 and the blue pod is Pod 3.

Behind the blue pod, there are only 2 pods left. Since the black pod and the red pod are both behind the blue one, and the black one is in front of the red one, the red pod must be Pod 5.

The correct answer is D.

How Many Pages?

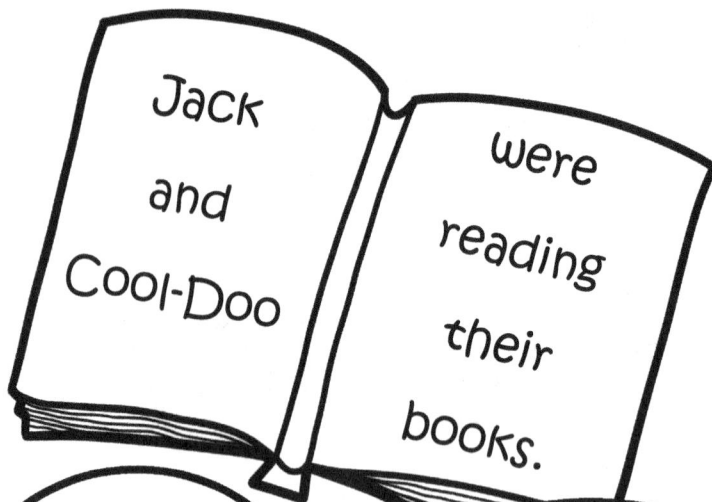

Jack and Cool-Doo were reading their books.

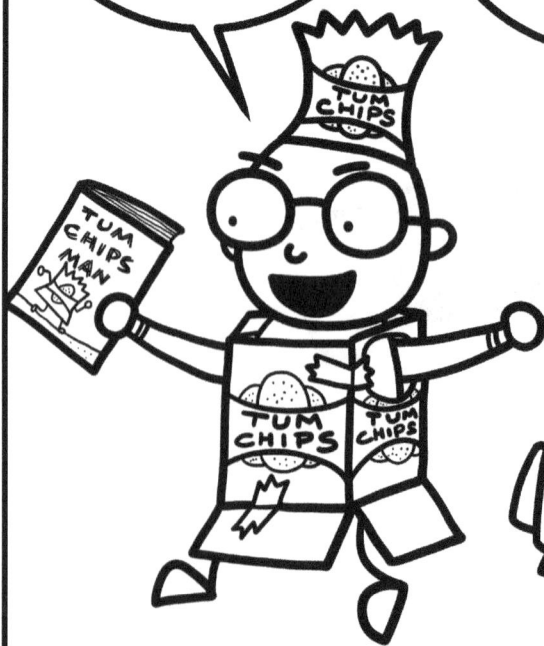

Beat him, TUM Chips Man!

I guess costumes aren't so bad after all.

So far I read all the pages before page 51.

So far I read all the pages before page 40.

I'm wondering what's the sum of the pages we have read and who is faster?

I think I read much faster than that Jack does.

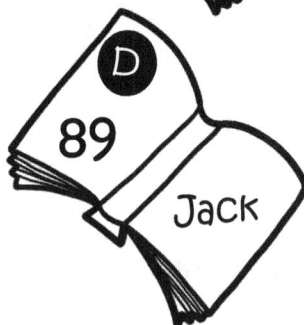

ANSWER

SOLUTION

Jack reads all the pages before page 51, so he reads 50 pages.

Cool-Doo reads all the pages before page 40, so he reads 39 pages.

Altogether, they read 50 + 39 = 89 pages.

Apparently, Jack reads more pages.

The correct answer is D.

About the Author

by Andrew, 2007

Andrew Feng

"Myths can be true; fairy tales can be true; even lies can be true. So, why not my dreams?"

Who made up this quote?

Andrew Feng did!

Born on a snowy day, he has always loved drawing doodles from his imagination, whether it's about ordinary Joes traveling around the world or extraordinary guys trying to defeat super villains.

Now, he enjoys drawing comics, reading, writing, swiming, playing the guitar, table tennis, tennis, and basketball, all with his best buddies.

Andrew is not sure what to be when he grows up, but he does know one thing — he will be an awesordinary (awesome + ordinary) guy!

I LoVE You Dad

by Adrew , 2007

Peter Feng

Peter is a realtor working in Great Tronto Area. He is neither a writer nor a professional illustrator. English is not even his first language. In 2008, his wife had a miscarriage that made his son Andrew very upset because he always dreamed of having a little brother. To cheer up his son, Peter created an imaginary brother Cool-Doo for Andrew and started creating Cool-Doo stories together with him. With the passion for creating a new family tradition, Peter and his son started learning creative writing from books, the Internet, teachers, writers and editors. With the help and support of family, friends and professional editors, Peter and Andrew published a children's novel, *TUM — The Unmoved Mover,* and a math comic series, *Cool-Doo Math.*

Peter loves the unmeasured, vast expanse of the ocean. He always sees himself as a sailor in the crow's nest looking beyond the horizon, a sailor who never gives up exploring and searching for a new continent.

by Adrew , 2009

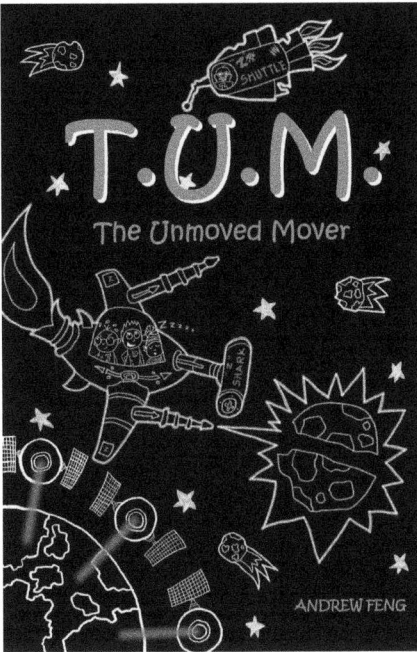

Do you get along with your brother?

Jack doesn't!

Although he has always expected to have a brother to play with, he finds his dream of brotherhood shattered after he gets a really "special" one. This special one always impresses Jack's parents. Plus, this special one also has a special friend of his own, and things always stir up crazily.

Finally, a chance comes for Jack to impress his parents. His hometown is placed in danger while he and the other two special guys are in a space camp, and he only has one night left to become the hero. But, of course, his "special" brother also wants to be the hero.

The clock is ticking...can they make it?

(www.t-u-m.net)

"*A **lively** adventure that **charms** and **delights!***"

- KIRKUS REVIEWS

Another Fun Book by Andrew Feng & Peter Feng

Rewriting fables is a very popular practice of creative writing, especially for kids. The process helps children analyze existing fables, think outside of the box to make a new story, and put what they see in their heads onto paper in an ordered, clear, and concise way.

How to Rewrite Fables in a TUM Way uses a comic story to take kids on an exciting and funny journey to learn the process of rewriting fables. Readers will learn the basic structure of a story and how to dressup their writing in a fun way. It also contains examples of rewritten fables.

The characters in the comic story are Jack, Cool-Doo, Sleepy-Doo, and Dr. Green, who are the main characters from the children's novel TUM - The Unmoved Mover.Visit www.t-u-m.net for more information.

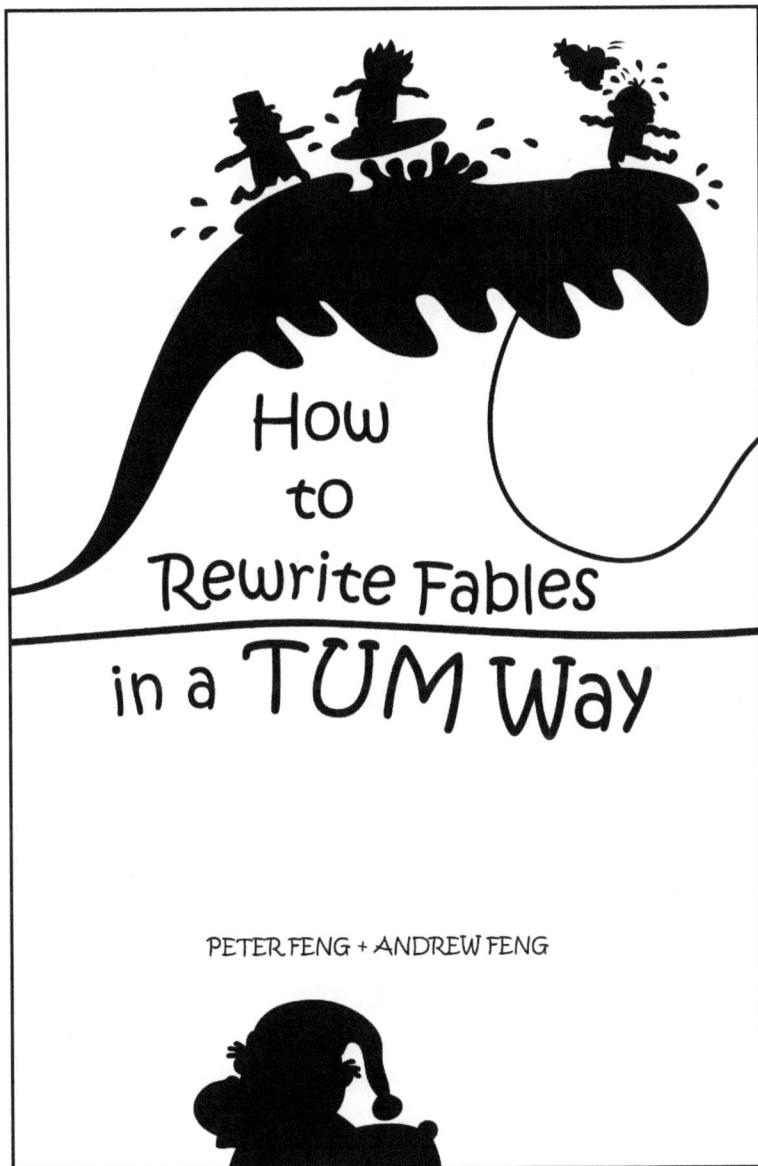

How to Rewrite Fables in a TUM Way

PETER FENG + ANDREW FENG

www.ingramcontent.com/pod-product-compliance
Lightning Source LLC
Chambersburg PA
CBHW061147040426
42445CB00013B/1590